Bibliographic information published by the German National Library:

The German National Library lists this publication in the National Bibliography; detailed bibliographic data are available on the Internet at http://dnb.dnb.de .

Imprint:

Copyright © 2017 GRIN Verlag, Open Publishing GmbH
Print and binding: Books on Demand GmbH, Norderstedt Germany
ISBN: 9783668455870

This book at GRIN:

http://www.grin.com/en/e-book/366386/organisational-change-and-its-reasons

Aruzhan Zhomart

Organisational Change and its Reasons

GRIN Publishing

GRIN - Your knowledge has value

Since its foundation in 1998, GRIN has specialized in publishing academic texts by students, college teachers and other academics as e-book and printed book. The website www.grin.com is an ideal platform for presenting term papers, final papers, scientific essays, dissertations and specialist books.

Visit us on the internet:

http://www.grin.com/

http://www.facebook.com/grincom

http://www.twitter.com/grin_com

Worldwide climate of economical and political instability and turbulence made change an inevitable part of any healthy organisation in society. Even company with dominant position in its market such as Apple after introduction of iPad has always to innovate and keep their products up-to-date (Robbins & Judge, 2013). Simplistically change means making things in a different way. Currently change is studied on the individual, group, national and multinational levels during different time periods, from days to years (Mullins, 2006).

Organisational change is a process when companies modify working methods, organisational structure and culture, mission and vision in order to survive, develop and cope with faced problems or situations (Robbins & Judge, 2013). According to Fincham and Rhodes (2005), change management is the leadership of the organisational change process, which includes important factor of minimizing change barriers.

The need for organisational change can be driven by lots of external and internal forces. According to Buchanan and Huczynski (2008), triggers of change are factors indicating that current organisational structure, procedures and working processes do not work towards the organisational success. External forces for change such as unstable economic conditions, technological advances, globalisation and political events originate outside the organisation, whilst internal forces such as changing nature of workforce, 'Quality approach' and social trends come within the organisation (Kreitner & Kinicki, 2010). Interestingly, organisational change often is initiated within the company, whereas the most of triggers come outside the organisation (Mullins, 2006). Unstable economic conditions are one of the external forces, which can create a volatile environment. For example, collapse of financial and housing markets in 2008 in the USA caused the global recession so demand for normal goods decreased, and companies in order to survive were forced to lower supply and create more affordable products. Another external driver of change is technological developments. Many organisations use technological advances as a tool to increase productivity, customer service, saving costs at the same time. For instance, there are more and more options of self-service from the Internet banks to grocery retailers. In 2008, for visitors of Adour Alain restaurant in New York there was offered a new option to order wine by tablet in order to increase the quality of customer service and add to give enjoy for visitors by learning about wines by choosing country or origin and wine extract (Ante, 2008). Globalisation of markets and the internationalisation of business is powerful external driver of change as it forced many companies to integrate, compete and use outsourcing to lower production costs (Mullins, 2006). Political events are considered as external forces of change as well. For instance, war in Iraq created job places for contractors and organisations like Halliburton (Kreitner & Kinicki, 2010).

One of the most broad internal trigger is changing nature of the workforce as under the effect of globalisation it became more culturally diversified, also caused by demographic issues as ageing population and increased immigration (Robbins & Judge, 2013). Social trends become popular trigger for change. Example how social trends drive the change is global concern about greenhouse effect and rising energy costs, which forced many industries to change. Moreover, Microsoft employees began to use free shuttle bus to go to work rather than use their own cars, they saved more than $1 billion during the first year only (Kreitner & Kinicki, 2010). In addition, due to flexibility in organisational structure many organisations are becoming 'flatter' in order to ensure better communication and effectively manage change. Another important trigger of change is 'Quality approach' or known as Kaizen concept of continuous improvement, which is based on increased demand from customers for high-quality good and satisfaction. Consequently it forced many organisations to seek customer feedback about various issues within their organisation. As example, through consumer feedback McDonalds identifies consumers' tastes and preferences and then changes menu (Kreitner & Kinicki, 2010). Low performance, high staff turnover (Buchanan, 2008) and organisational conflict (Mullins, 2006) are also considered as internal forces for change.

As with any change there are some risks and rewards. Spectrum of organisational change consists of 4 types of change known as automation, rationalization, reengineering and paradigm shift. Automation and rationalization are related to incremental (evolutionary) changes as the present modest returns and low risks, whereas reengineering and paradigm shift are related to transformational changes and offer high rewards, however with high probability of failure. Incremental adjustment involves many small unplanned changes such as modifications to business planning and management processes, whilst transformational change includes change in the way of thinking, solution of problems, defining boundaries and doing business. For example, banks may decide to use revolutionary change and eliminate branch banking, whereas IT companies prefer automation and rationalization implementing incremental changes (Burnes & James, 1995).

According to Robbins and Judge (2013), all theoretical approaches for change management are based on planned change, which is intentional and task oriented. When it comes to plan and implement change the fundamental technique was developed by Lewin (1951) who suggested 3-step Behaviour Modification technique. These stages are unfreezing the status quo (equilibrium state), movement to a desired state and refreezing change to make it permanent. During the unfreezing change agents identify initial problem and gather necessary data. The key point of this stage is motivation creation for change. Change agents try to persuade people to replace old working methods, attitudes by innovative and desired by management (Kreitner and Kinicki, 2010). In the 'unfreezing' stage managers identify key reason of change and prepare employees to modification process. During the movement stage change takes place. Managers introduce new information, procedure, equipment, technology or new view on culture and structure. The aim of this stage is supporting and stabilizing implemented changes. Support for workers is provided by helping them to combine implemented processes with past formal way of working. Monetary rewards is commonly used practice during this stage of change for employees who show performance and willingness to change.

Despite the fact that it is theoretical approach, there are some assumptions to undertake for real world usage (Kreitner&Kinicki, 2010). Firstly, change process requires quitting some organisational processes or behaviour. Secondly, it is crucial to understand that unless there is no motivation, change will not happen. Finding real motivation is one the most difficult parts of change. Finally, people are the center of attention of change process so any change begins from individual level.

Lewin considered that it would be easier to increase effectiveness of organisational change process by focusing on communication and employee involvement (Akan, 2008). Moving on to the study of successful change management process, which took place in Remploy based on Lewin's model (Jessop, 2008). Remploy is the company, which provides employment for disabled people in the UK. As a consequence of recession managers understood that for the cost of employing one worker in Remploy they could have found four jobs in another place, so change was inevitable. Therefore, they decided to close the half of 83 UK factories. According to Force Field Theory in order to move from status quo managers began to decrease restraining forces such as unions, which mounted many political campaigns. So communication, participation and support were very important parts of minimizing resistance. Firstly, by the help of company Penna there were more than 4000 individual consultation meetings to support workers. Secondly, Penna consultants offered different opportunities for employees such as movement to other Remploy factory or working for another local employer. Thirdly, employees were informed and involved at each stage of change. Once unfreezing was successful, managers moved to changing stage. During movement 68% of disabled employees chose voluntary redundancy, 14% transferred to other Remploy factories and 18% stayed. Moreover, due to active communication 15 fewer companies were closed and Remploy improved their financial performance. At the last stage of change process Penna consultants were stabilizing implemented changes and supporting disabled employees to combine new practices with their past way of working.

Although there are successful cases of change processes based on Lewin's three step model, his work was increasingly criticized from the 1980s as it is relevant only to small-scale changes in stable conditions, and for ignoring issues such as organisational politics and conflict. (Dawson, 1994). Moreover, Kanter (1992) criticized Lewin's approach as too simplistic for constanly changing organisational processes.

Another powerful technique for implementing change is Kotter's Eight-Step Model (1996). His approach is based on Lewin's three-step model, but it is more detailed. He suggests beginning change by listing common mistakes, which management makes when they try to initiate change.

The case study of Corus shows how successfully implemented can be Kotter's model. Corus is one of the biggest steel i manufactures in the UK. Kotter's first 4 steps reflect Lewin's unfreezing stage. At first step managers identify a significant reason for change. In case with Corus it was high competition from low cost producers and staff morale, especially after tragic accident occurred with employee due working process. At the second step of change process there was created powerful guiding coalition headed by Managing Director. At the third step coalition developed a new vision 'to be leader in the steel industry by providing better products, higher quality customer service and better value for money than its rivals'. New values such as honesty, integrity, professionalism and excellence were introduced for employees (The Times, 2008). In order to communication the change vision company shared with employees what will happen if change does not occur. Through the direct and indirect communication strategy employees were more involved in decision making. In addition, Corus appointed weekly workshops and newsletters to ensure employees what was happening. Steps 5, 6 and 7 represent 'movement stage'. Step 5 includes getting rid of resistances to change by allowing people to take risk. For step 6 managers generate short-term wins for employees and create rewards, so Corus paid attention on employees accepting assistance to improve performance and rewarded them. At the seventh stage change was implemented, which focused in commitment of employees and looking for solution to problems such as cutting staff or investing in new equipment. Finally, changes were reinforced by around 150 workshops and newspapers clarified new introduced values and changes. As a result during 2-year change period Corus achieved great success and included 20% decrease in cost of steel production, health and safety conditions were improved in order to avoid accidents during working process and production capacity increased by 4.5%.

However, according to Dawson (1994), important disadvantage of Kotter's approach is that the it does not take into consideration the constant changes in the global economy, and that it fails to do so by laying out a linear roadmap to change, rather than a cyclical one. Interestingly, Kotter (1995) gave a response that his model was not created to manage all types of change; it was projected to manage "fundamental changes in how the business is conducted in order to help cope with a new, more challenging market environment".

However, even effective change processes occur, there always be resistance in any organisation as it is the natural reaction on change. Resistance originates from two levels: individual and organisational. Kotter and Schlesinger (1979) identified four main reasons of resistances on individual level. Firstly, it is parochial self-interest, when employees more think about their personal interests rather than the success of organisation. The second reason is misunderstanding caused by poor communication. Third reason is low tolerance to change caused by workers who are keen on security. The fourth reason is different assessments of the situation (selective information processing), which is related to keeping subjective perceptions.

Particularly resistance to change on organisational level Katz and Kahn (1978) suggests that the reasons come from narrow focus of change (one division cannot be changed without affecting other), resource allocation, group inertia (when individuals are ready to change, but organisational norms of behaviour are constraints) and threatened power (senior managers may lose their power so they resist change).

In order to overcome, prevent and minimize all aforementioned resistances to change Kotter and Schlesinger (1979) created six methods. The first is education and communication, which is used when there is misunderstanding or inaccurate information. It may be beneficial for organisation as people were encouraged, then they will often help with implementation of change and come back with new ideas for organisation performance, however it may be very time consuming if a big group of workers is involved. The second approach is participation and involvement. It is used when resistance is caused by fear of unknown, advantage of this method is fear reduction and as employees are involved they will support change. Unfortunately this method is also time-consuming. The next method is facilitation and support, which is the best working approach when anxiety over personal impact is the core reason of resistance. Disadvantages are time-consuming, expensiveness and it still may fail. The fourth measure is negotiation and agreement, which is used when stakeholders' or Board members' interests were threatened, sometimes it is easy way to prevent resistance, but usually it is very expensive way and may persuade others to strike deals. The fifth way is manipulation and co-optation, it is used when no of aforementioned can successfully implement change other approaches will not work within the organisation or are too expensive and time-consuming, however in future it can cause problems if people know that they were manipulated. The final approach is coercion, appropriate when change must be implemented fast. Besides it is very risky way used as a last resort.

In addition, managers can manage resistance to change on the basis of Maslow's Needs Theory. Once psychological and security needs are met, employees want to satisfy their social and self esteem needs such as nice office or recognition from colleagues. When employees reach all 5 levels of needs with self-actualization they become interested in growth of organisation, that is why it is very important to give employees opportunities for personal development, hence in future they will contribute the organisational performance. Moreover, in order to cope with resistance, managers should stop using mushroom management style, if they want to achieve success through change.

To sum up, this paper aimed to explain how organisations use change management techniques in order to achieve performance and success of company through employee participation and how internal and external forces drive the change process. Firstly, based on the definitions of change management and organisational change, the key external and internal forces primarily identified, which drive the change. In terms of application of the most powerful and influential change models by Lewin (1951) and Kotter (1995), there were demonstrated successful case studies of Remploy and Corus companies where managers successfully implemented the change based on these approaches. Despite the fact that Lewin's three step model is highly criticized, Lewin's ideas are fundamental and pioneer for successful planned change as all other approaches such as Kotter's eight-step plan, organisational development and appreciative enquiry are based on Lewin. With reference to 'human relations', Lewin considered that a positive employee attitude to change and participation is vital for successful result. In support to Lewin, Tan and Tiong (2005) suggested that the optimism or attitude to change was the most important success factor for change.

References:

Akan O. H. and Medley B. C. (2008) 'Creating Positive Change in Community Organizations', Nonprofit Management and Leadership, 18(4), pp. 485-496

Ante E. S. (2008) The iSommelier Will Take Your Order. Available at: https://www.bloomberg.com/news/articles/2008-02-13/the-isommelier-will-take-your-order (Accesed at: 3 January 2017).

Buchanan, D. and Huczynski, A. (2006) *Organizational Behaviour*, 7th edition. Harlow: FT/Prentice Hall.

Burnes, B. and James, H. (1995) 'Culture, cognitive dissonance and the management of change', International Journal of Operations & Production Management, 15(8), pp. 14-33.

Cameron, E. and Green M. (2015) 'Making Sense of Change Management', 4th edition. London and Philadelphia: Kogan Page.

Dawson, P. (1994) *Organizational Change: A Processual Approach.* London: Paul Chapman Publishing.

Dunphy, D. and Stace, D., (1993) 'The strategic management of corporate change', Human Relations, 46(8), pp. 16-19.

Jessop, A. (2008) 'How I made a difference at work', People Management, 14(12):44

Katz, D. and Kahn, R. (1978) The Social Psychology or Organizations, 2nd edition. Michigan: John Wiley & Sons.

Kotter, J.P. and Schlesinger, L. A (1979) 'Choosing strategies for change', Harvard Business Review, 57(2), pp. 106–114.

Kotter, J.P. (1995) 'Leading Change: Why Transformation Efforts Fail', Harvard Business Review, 73(2), pp. 59-67.

Lewin, C. (1951) Frontiers in Group Dynamics. Field Theory in Social Change. New York (USA), Harper and Row Publishers.

Kinitcki A. and Kreitner R. (2010). Organizational Behavior, 9th edition. New York: McGraw-Hill.

Kanter, R.M., B. Stein. (1992). The Challenge or Organisational Change: How Companies Experience it and Leaders. New York: Free Press.

Mullins L. J. (2008). Essentials of Organisational Behaviour, 2nd edition. Harlow: FT/Prentice Hall.

Robbins P. S. and Judge A. T. (2013). Organizational Behavior, 15th edition. Pearson: FT Prentice Hall.

Tan, V., & Tiong, T. N. (2005) 'Change management in times of economic uncertainty', Singapore Management Review, 27, pp. 49-68.

Scholes, K. (2008) 'Overcoming barriers to change: a Corus case study' Available at: http://businesscasestudies.co.uk/corus/overcoming-barriers-to-change/introduction.html#axzz4VNS1Kv82 (Accesed at: 10 January 2017).

Song X. (2009). 'Why Do Change Management Strategies Fail? Illustrations with case studies', Journal of Cambridge Studies, 4(1), pp. 6-15.

Fincham R. and Rhodes P. (2005). Principles of Organizational Behaviour, 4th edition. Oxford: Oxford University Press.